RAILS

Books by Don Ball, Jr.

Portrait of the Rails

Railroads: An American Journey

Decade of the Trains: The 1940's

America's Colorful Railroads

America's Railroads: The Second Generation

Rails

RAILS

DON BALL, Jr.

Designed by Hugh O'Neill

W. W. NORTON & COMPANY • NEW YORK • LONDON

Published simultaneously in Canada by George J. McLeod Limited, Toronto.
Printed in the United States of America
All Rights Reserved
First Edition

W. W. Norton & Company, Inc. 500 Fifth Avenue, New York, N.Y. 10110
W. W. Norton & Company Ltd., 37 Great Russell Street, London WC1B 3NU
ISBN 0 393 01480 0
1 2 3 4 5 6 7 8 9 0

TO WALT_____

For years my close friend Walt Grosselfinger
has been encouraging me to do a book of my work alone.
I hope this meets with his approval.

Editor's Foreword

About a year ago Don Ball and I were talking about photography. We were looking at a particularly arresting photograph in a book by our mutual friend David Plowden when Don said that he had taken one similar to it. I asked to see it. A few days later he brought it into my office along with about a dozen others. I had never seen any of them, and I was stunned. In front of me were some of the strongest black-and-white photographs I'd ever seen. All were of railroad subjects but often not sufficiently detailed or in other ways suitable for Don's usual documentary books. Therefore, they had not been reproduced. But they were so beautiful and evocative that I pestered him for more with the thought of publishing a book that would do them justice. Over the next few months Don brought carloads of enlargements and contact sheets into my office. Visitors and colleagues were equally impressed with them. I began to select what I felt were the finest shots, without regard to subjects, dates, or locations. *Rails* is the result, a new and different Don Ball book. While a few of the photographs in this volume have been reproduced before, I felt they deserved better treatment. And, of course, I've undoubtedly missed some that others might have chosen. Nevertheless, the black-and-white photographs reproduced here have convinced me that Don Ball, Jr. is one of our finest photographers. I hope they bring as much pleasure to others as they have to me.

Jim Mairs
July 1981

RAILS

"HEY, RED, go on down the tracks past those boxcars and we'll give you a show!" With the cord of my Brownie Reflex carefully wrapped around my wrist, I did what the engineer said and ran down past the Derby Diet grain elevator, the two boxcars, and up beyond the next crossing. The headlight on the big Rock Island 4-8-4 stared right at me, and I could see the fireman moving around on top of the tender. The fireman pushed the big water plug spout away from the tender back to its normal standing position, and I knew "the show" was about to begin. #5064's whistle shouted two times, and it was offically under way! The bell-ringer valve opened, steam roared from the big engine's cylinder cocks as the first chuff of steam bellowed into the clear summer air. 5064 immediately put her shoulder into it all. Her voice was accompanied by white chuffs of steam blasting out of the stack in quick succession. The white turned to gray and then black, curling up into the dead-still Kansas air. The big Northern was pulling hard to overcome the inertia of the once-standing train. My eyes turned to the view finder, and I watched carefully as the noisy #5064 loomed large. Clearly, the smoke was too high to catch on film. I tripped the shutter moments before the beautiful engine shook the ground going by, both crewmen waving from the right side of the cab. The cars that followed were temporarily eclipsed by 5064's dark cumulus exhaust, and I concentrated on the shiny steel wheels' symphonic *click-clack* over the heavy rails. The loaded cars continued to clomp on by while 5064's onslaught was still clearly heard leading the parade out of town. The brown wooden hack brought up the rear with the tinkling crossing bells ceasing, street by street, in the train's wake. The whistle called for the Bismarck Grove crossing. That day I documented something on film that was special to me, breathtaking to an eight year old! There would be other trains and plenty of other pictures, each different, but few would capture the profound sense of excitement I felt that day with my Brownie.

To this day, I remain relatively naïve when it comes to the technical aspects of photography. Probably my little Brownie Reflex had a shutter speed somewhere around 1/60 second, so the moving trains were always blurred (as, in many cases, I remember certain trains were, when rushing past!), but at eight years of age, that did not bother me. I can plainly see that I was shooting right into the sun on many occasions—but wasn't I looking right into the sun, watching the train? Technicalities…Capturing the moment that excited me was all that mattered. Now, and almost four decades later, I still can look at the original deckle-edged jumbo prints in the little photo-album booklets and recall my boyhood excitement.

Several years after my first shots, I saw some 8 x 10 black-and-white glossy photographs that a friend had taken of trains, and a whole new world was opened up to me. The clarity of detail—especially of a moving train—really impressed me, and I realized what I was *not getting* with my own camera. I could immediately see that the little snapshots not only were not sharp, but totally lacked the contrast that showed the punch and power of the trains. It was obvious that I had to buy a "good camera." This became an immediate and all-compelling objective.

The era of the one-inch square 127 negatives came to an end late in 1951 with the purchase of a used circa 1934 Rolliflex Model T with a Tessar 3.5 lens. The dealer told me about exposures—the relation between F stop and shutter speed, depth of field, and other technicalities. I was relieved when he loaded the camera with some 120 Verichrome Pan (more on films later) and jotted down some "typical sunny-weather exposure settings" for the day. Off to the depot I went.

My first exposure was of the westbound *Texas Rocket*'s TA diesel, sort of framed next to—really kind of behind—the water plug. Another shot that day was made of a fast-moving UP 2-10-2 passing through town, broadside at 1/125 second. These were the highlights on that first roll of film. After twelve exposures I eagerly returned to Hixon's Camera Studio to have the film removed from the camera for developing. I had seen some exciting action—as I usually did—but this time, I had *the* camera to catch what I saw. Great expectations…When I picked up the roll of film two days later, I was in for a shock. The prints were sharp, but I clearly had "blown it!" The clarity emphasized everything, including what I should not have done. Perhaps intuitively, I did sense what I *should* have done. One way or another, I could see that the train's action had to be stopped with more or less regular assurance! The 1/125 second did not do the job. The composition—or lack of it—was clear, as were the contrasty shots against the sun. Light and shadow were things I was going to have to reckon with from now on. With the Rolliflex, I clearly could see that I had an instrument capable of documenting many of the exciting moments that I wanted to preserve, but my work was cut out for me. I knew I had to master the camera.

Then, as now, there were moments that I experienced, moments I'll always remember, that I would have loved to have preserved, but never could. Images, like the Rock Island *Golden State Limited* on a warm summer night, approaching town—its important big new EMD diesels throttling down for the station stop sometime near midnight—headlight shining down the track and then looming on up past the waiting people on the platform, each unit's six-wheel truck *thump-thump-thumping* over the rail joints, followed by head end car after head end car, fanning up the smells of hot grease and oil, and brake shoes, until the Pullmans rolled up, their porters shining the handrails as the cars came to a smooth stop, the porters, almost as if choreographed, swinging down to the platform, planting foot stools in front of the steps. And inside the great cars, people bedding down or sleeping in the dark rooms, most of the shades drawn tight—a dark line punctuated by an occasional bright window of a room ready to be occupied or just vacated by people getting off. The hubbub of tired greetings and soft embraces, the firm-voiced "This car to Chicago." There's a wonderful moment of pure enchantment, watching the great train, drinking it all in, and, yes, wishing I could preserve this magic on film. A commanding *"Booaarrd"* is heard from the rear of the train. Through the darkness, the conductors' highball is signaled on toward the head end with the flashlights of trainmen; the engineer quickly acknowledging the highball with two blasts on the air horns and an immediate latching out of 6,000 horsepower. One quickly senses that the Rock Island's brass back in Chicago are watching closely as the traps are punctually closed, porters start tending to their passengers, and trainmen watch from vestibules, as the *Golden State* makes its rapid departure—dead on time—out of Lawrence. The markers bring up the rear of the departing train, and once again the dark takes over. To this day, I wish all of this wonderment could be documented in photographs. Certainly, the mind's eye is a marvelous possession.

Two years after I bought the Rollei, I made fast friends with a guy who had built a darkroom and was into the world of developing and printing his black-and-white stuff. His darkroom was certainly not a fancy setup, but enough to give me a "feel" for developing and printing—especially printing (enlarging). Once again, a whole new world was opened up to me as I eagerly watched and picked up as much as possible while I had the chance. Many an hour was spent "making pictures" (and I have a reason for calling it that) with my buddy's Kodak Hobbyist enlarger from my little 127 negatives and, of course, the larger 120-size negatives.

Now, I'd like to comment on what I mean by "making pictures." Quite simply, and for the first time in my life, I could take a negative, print it, and *then* see better ways of bringing out more "feel" in the next print. I could take a negative (especially the larger, clearer 120 negative) and print it, cropping out what I felt was not pertinent to the focal point—or strength—leaving out the peripheral portion that detracted from the main point of interest. I could also add or dodge the darks and lights to change, or add to, the mood. Needless to say, a lot of paper was expended as I more or less "taught myself" to make enlargements to my satisfaction. The enlarger clearly became the tool—or eye—to express on paper what I wanted. (In later years, the camera would become the on-the-spot tool—or eye—to *catch* what I knew I would want in a picture.) Developing the film was pure drudgery (I have long since turned to labs to do the developing), but printing made it all worth-while. Soon, I bought a used Omega D-2 enlarger and set up a very primitive darkroom, using a board over the bathtub in the bathroom (something I still do!).

I am convinced that all my photographic skills have been acquired in reverse order from the norm. For example, in 1955, I started using my school's 4 x 5 Crown graphic with a Schneider Compor F1:4.7 lens. At first, I did not take too kindly to the camera's bulk, film packs, etc.—nor to the fact I could take only one picture of a passing train with the camera. I was used to taking a distant shot, the close-up shot, and then the passing shot of any train I would wait for. Now, however, the 4 x 5 forced me into *composing* the one picture I would be taking. I was enchanted by the great, clear negatives the 4 x 5 offered and gladly gave up the flexibility in order to get that "one luscious negative." The 4 x 5 made me look for the best picture I could get, knowing I only had one crack at the train—distant, close up, or going away. Things like the angle of light and location of other objects quickly became very important to me. The 4 x 5 really taught me to look at what I would be taking a picture of—in effect "making the picture" first and then documenting it with the camera. A turning point was reached when I could take a picture, knowing I either got, or didn't get what I would be looking for in the darkroom, printing the photograph from the negative. What used to go unnoticed in a picture soon became the elements to be included in the picture!

In 1960 I purchased a secondhand Hasselblad 1000F with an 80-mm Tessar 1:2.8 lens after briefly using a 2¼ x 3¼ Kodak Medalist. I had long since gone back to the Rolliflex's square-format negative soon after my initial bout with the 4 x 5, preferring its 2¼-square-inch size to the 4 x 5. (Ironically, while it was the 4 x 5 that taught me composition, it was the 2¼-square format I felt most comfortable with.) With a little practice in the darkroom, I found that I could get good enough negatives from the Rollei and at the same time get the convenience of having an easier-to-handle camera back. The days of the 4 x 5 were over. The Hasselblad offered a *system* of interchangeable lenses and film backs, and it was at this point that I made a definite decision to *document* and not *create* with the camera. Documenting what I saw was clearly the focus for me in photography (bad pun!), and I snubbed the telephoto and wide-angle lenses (something I still do), which I felt were good for *creating* and not *documenting*.

We are talking about 1960, a crucial year and turning point for me and photography. Up until 1960, my world of photography was one of capturing—documenting—the great, wonderful, showful steam locomotives across our nation's rails and, as I've pointed out in previous books, wearing out cameras and cars in the cross-country chasing process! Why, every time you watched a steam locomotive, the shapes and patterns of its smoke and steam were different, and no two pictures of a working locomotive were ever the same. The machines were alive! The visual impression of a steam locomotive's power was indeed eloquent and needed only to be photographed to be preserved. Not so with the diesels that, incidentally, totally replaced all main-line steam operations in 1960. Photographing a diesel at 80 miles an hour—stopping it dead on its track at 1/1,000 second—might just as well have been photographing the train sitting in a railroad yard. Absent were the smoke and steam billowing over the engine and train's movement. And once more, with the exception of paint schemes, the internal-combustion creatures all looked about the same. True, there were different kinds and different manufacturers of diesels, but the visual pomp and ceremony of steam was gone. No longer would the act of merely documenting an engine with good cameras assure exciting results. A diesel is a diesel is a diesel...

In 1960, with main-line steam now vanished from the rails, the choice was one of putting the camera away or, somehow, sticking with the railroad scene, diesels and all. Notice I said *railroad scene* and not merely the engines and trains. The diesel was a challenge to the photographer, and one had to "work" at making a scene with 'em in it exciting. In 1960, I *did* shelve the camera as far as rail photography went, but a curious thing soon happened. As always, *Trains* magazine arrived in the mail. Little by little, the contemporary railroad pictures started to appear in the magazine's "Photo Section," and I soon realized that the contemporary pictures were getting more interesting in their content and overall composition. It was obvious that the diesels were forcing rail photographers into creating better pictures by portraying not only the diesel, but the *total railroad habitat* in which the diesel worked. By 1964 I was back at trackside dealing not only with the diesel, but the *total railroad scene.* Some of the images in this book attest to that fact.

Today, because of my boyhood love for trains, I am an avid photographer—whether photographing landscapes, architecture, people, aircraft, or trains. Nineteen sixty was the year that I gave up what got me into photography—but not the photography!

The photographs in this book are a sampling of the tens of thousands of rail-related images I have made on film—most of the "nonlocomotive pictures" having been taken since 1960. My last two books *were* in color, but black-and-white photography, to me, still offers the greatest opportunity to achieve—yes, document—on paper one's true visual experience or feeling at the time the exposure was made. *Learning to see the picture first* is the key, I think, to the successful translation of what you want to document onto a negative. Learning to be aware of things around you, seeing things you haven't seen before—and knowing it at the time! Carefully analyzing the subject you want to document again and again and recognizing the elements that make the picture *before* taking the picture! (With trains, of course, the real sport is to visualize the introduction of the train into the scene *before* the train comes, knowing how to "work the elements" to advantage.) Photography is communicating what you see and, perhaps more important, how you feel about what you see.

Photography, to me, is also successfully documenting *total impressions,* usually emphasized by portraying the subject in its most acknowledged natural or most widely thought of habitat: I mean a Metroliner—flat out—racing down the New York–Washington corridor in the late afternoon; hazy sun through muggy, polluted air, under wires, between catenary poles—in a steel and cement world—without a trace of nature's life...an ex-Texas & Pacific Texas–type

2-10-4 in Texas—clearly the only place to shoot this critter—where grass and phone poles and everything in between are silhouetted against the miles and miles of endless miles. Texas for a Texan...the Baltimore & Ohio's heavy steel rails slicing through historic Harpers Ferry, through the mountains, next to where the Potomac and Shenandoah rivers join in their confrontaton with the Blue Ridge, forcing the railroad up on bridges...the mighty Union Pacific crossing the continent, ganging up on the forever flatlands of barren Wyoming with no less than three E-8s and a 4-8-4 on the *San Francisco Overland,* outrunning a towering thunderstorm that's as awesome as the land the train is racing over...the Pennsylvania Railroad, antithesized by the grime and darkness of the Northumberland, Pennsylvania, roundhouse, whose cinder-deep worn rails lead out to the turntable and a grunty I-1, being turned for its next battle along the Mesabi rust-covered Shamokin branch in a drizzling rain...the Burlington Route—the far-flung railroad that sired the sleek, streamlined *Zephyr* back in 1934 and then went on to build a fleet of newer and better *Zephyrs*; a vision of 100-mph vista-domed silver trains. Nothing else than intentionally blurred E units lunging down the Chicago-Aurora race track with the *Denver Zephyr* would do—and mind you, I'm talking about blurring a train at 1/250 of a second!...the main line of the mighty New York Central in the historic Hudson highlands, where silver streamliners and fast-moving freights whiz past the abandoned stone quarries of years past. Through a window in the old powerhouse, the silent silos line up the side of Mt. Thaurus, and, in the silent absence of a train, one can only imagine the thud and clatter of the belts and the sorters...the sheer size of railroad equipment itself—quintessentially ugly and grotesquely massive to some while visually intense and aesthetically compelling to others. The strength and functionality that make up the individual components of the railroad fancifully viewed in the rail-level shot of standing wheels and axles in Western Pacific's Portola, California, yard...the dream and drama of rebuilding a long-time-out-of-service steam locomotive for a new and purposeful life out on the rails—an example being the Steam Locomotive Corporation of America's total reincarnation of the ex–Chesapeake & Ohio Greenbrier #614. Where else, and how else can the total story be told than on fire-up day in the Western Maryland Hagerstown roundhouse, seconds before the huge 4-8-4 is moved out under her own steam for her test run? Total impressions...

I have avoided any comment on the technicalities of photography—and with good reason. For better or for worse, what I do in the darkroom (or with a camera) is nothing more than expressing myself. I have not read "how to do it" books on photography, nor have I had formal instruction on the subject. What I do, I have picked up largely by trial and error—and, yes, by "feel." I shy away from thermometers, test strips, and in general manage to violate every rule in the technical book! Close friends know I *still* get *overexposed* and *underexposed* mixed up! The one time I "listened" to a light meter over my own instinct, I blew the exposures! The dear Lord has provided me with a "built-in light meter" that I can trust, and Kodak has provided Tri-X film in lieu of the Verichrome Pan I used in the beginning.

I'd like to close with one more image from a camera that I have only briefly alluded to: we're out in the Blue Ridge Mountains on a summer night. The moonbeams are slanting through the silent pines and illuminating the open meadows in an eerie gray-white blanket, rendering the surrounding shadows impenetrable. Fireflies sparkle, on and off, everywhere, vying for attention with the diamond-bright stars overhead. The *zeet-zeet-zeet...zeet-zeet-zeet* of crickets is heard everywhere in a soft chorus. A short distance away, the twin steel ribbons of Norfolk & Western's well-burnished main line reflect the moonlight—silent. In the far-off distance a hooter whistle breaks the spell of the brilliant still air. For the next twenty minutes or so there is the increasing drama of a heavy coal train being lugged upgrade by two hard-working, volcanic-voiced, articulated steam locomotives. It will reach a climax with the shattering noise of two of Norfolk & Western's largest steam locomotives unleashing their power moving the heavy train upgrade. Their smoke and steam, etched in the moonlight, the wavering orange glow from the fireboxes adding unbelievable visual impact to the drama. All of this is punctuated by the black forms of the engines and the following train in the moonlight. As the engines pass by, I can imagine that this whole spectacle is an attempt to blow the night into pieces! The ground still shakes and trembles from the pounding of two million plus pounds, even after the slugging pair of behemoths thunder into the darkness. The drumming cadence of laden hopper cars—filled with coal, resisting the upward pull—rolls on and on, the cars casting their symmetrical outlines in the moonlight. The caboose appears and passes into the dark. And then it is over.

I can never adequately describe in words nor obviously commit to film scenes such as the above that have been clearly documented by the greatest "camera" of them all—my own mind (and memory!). The memories of such moments are, beyond a doubt, some of my most precious possessions, and it is only hoped that someday technical achievements in photography will even allow us to capture such wonderful images on film as the *Golden State Limited* leaving town or a Norfolk & Western coal train out on Blue Ridge.

Portrait of a Pennsylvania Railroad Class J—Columbus, Ohio.

Water tank at Strasburg, Pennsylvania.

5:00 A.M. call at Burlington's Clyde Yard, Chicago.

Union Pacific eastbound fruit block. Lawrence, Kansas.

Lunch break. New York Central at Harmon, New York.

Looking for rear end signals. Mid-Continent Railway Museum.

From the shanty. Northwestern Steel & Wire. Sterling, Illinois.

Pinch-hitting for the diesels. Pennsylvania K-4 at Tuscarora, Pennsylvania.

Water stop. Southern Railway—Charlottesville, Virginia.

Lima Super Power. Ex-Nickel Plate Road #759. Binghamton, New York.

Steam-era memories. Chesapeake & Ohio Yard—Charlottesville, Virginia.

Servicing a Burlington 0-5 at Clyde Yard, Chicago.

The climb over Sherman Hill, Wyoming on the Union Pacific.

Coal haulers. Reading Railroad T-1's at Shamokin, Pennsylvania.

World's largest. Union Pacific Big Boy drifting on Sherman Hill, Wyoming.

Iron Range behemoth. Duluth, Mesabi & Iron Range ore train.

Western horizons. Colorado & Southern northbound freight near Loveland, Colorado.

Departing Clyde roundhouse. Burlington route—Chicago.

Reincarnation of a giant. Ex–C&O #614, Hagerstown, Maryland.

Preparing for the run. Ex–Nickel Plate #759, Harmon, New York.

Gandy dancers. Union Pacific east of Grand Island, Nebraska.

Twilight of steam on the Western Maryland. Helmstetter's Curve, Maryland.

Getting out of the hole. Pennsylvania Railroad near Chattfield, Ohio.

Canadian National roundhouse. Hamilton, Ontario.

Steel mill. Northwestern Steel & Wire—Sterling, Illinois.

Baltimore and Ohio yard goat. Connellsville, Pennsylvania.

Assignment in the rain. Pennsylvania I-1—Northumberland, Pennsylvania.

Pacing a 2-10-4. Ex–Texas & Pacific #610 near Sunrise, Texas.

Highballing through Texas! Ex–Texas & Pacific #610 near Bowie, Texas.

The climb toward Widen. Buffalo, Creek & Gauley RR. West Virginia.

Baltimore & Ohio's morning local through St. Dennis, Maryland.

Crossing Wisconsin. Circus train near Lake Mills on the Chicago & Northwestern.

Arival at Effner, Indiana. Ex–NKP #765 on the Toledo, Peoria & Western.

Shop buildings. Western Maryland Railway. Hagerstown, Maryland.

Ready for the run. Ex–C&O #614 at Hagerstown, Maryland roundhouse.

Early-morning departure. Burlington 0-5 at Clyde Yard, Chicago.

Prelude to a blizzard. Union Pacific at Cheyenne, Wyoming.

Chicago bound. Burlington Railroad #4960 east of Aurora, Illinois.

Back lighting the Grand Trunk Western near Valparaiso, Indiana.

Running repairs. Ex–T&P #610 on Southern Railway near Orange, Virginia.

Rolling the high cars across Nevada on the Western Pacific.

Union Pacific Extra 9043 west. Lawrence, Kansas.

Westbound run. Ex–NKP #765 on the TP&W.

Departing Dundon. Buffalo, Creek & Gauley at Dundon, West Virginia.

Northern Pacific's *North Coast Limited* departing Missoula, Montana.

Highballing the beef. Pennsylvania Railroad eastbound near Longfellow, Pennsylvania.

Hotbox setoff. Chicago & Northwestern at Clinton, Iowa.

Thunder on the Overland Trail. Union Pacific at Borie, Wyoming.

Set off track. Northern Pacific Railway at Missoula, Montana.

The Chessie Steam Special assaulting Seventeen Mile Grade.

The Chessie Steam Special west of Keyser, West Virginia.

Extra UP-SP 8444 west, descending Donner Pass, California.

Leaking pump. Buffalo, Creek & Gauley 2-8-0 #14.

Indiana blizzard. Monon's southbound *Thoroughbred* at Greencastle, Indiana.

Monon's northbound *Thoroughbred* arriving at Greencastle, Indiana.

Southland departure. Seaboard Coast Line's *Silver Meteor* departing New York City.

Pennsylvania Railroad's *Congressional Limited* departing New York City.

Overnight snow. Green Mountain Railroad tracks at Bellows Falls, Vermont.

Wyoming blizzard. Union Pacific extra #8444 west on Sherman Hill.

Eastbound coal on the Union Pacific near Lawrence, Kansas.

Union Equity's grain elevator at Saginaw, Texas.

Coastal fog. New Haven Railroad—Cos Cob, Connecticut, drawbridge.

Tracks through history. Baltimore & Ohio Railroad at Harpers Ferry, West Virginia.

Under the bow arches. New Haven RR through Glenbrook, Connecticut.

View from the head end. Baltimore & Ohio Railroad near Hancock, West Virginia.

Westward dash. Burlington's Denver *Zephyr* near Lisle, Illinois.

Gotham-bound commuters. Conrail through Hawthorne, New York.

Back country. American Freedom Train test run near Camas, Washington.

Northeast courier. Amtrak's train no. 170 northbound through Darien, Connecticut.

New York Central RS-3 at North White Plains, New York.

New York Central RS-3 at North White Plains, New York.

Pennsylvania Railroad's *Duquesne* near Huntingdon, Pennsylvania.

Green Mountain Railroad caboose hop through Riverside, Vermont.

Into the night. Southern Railway's southbound *Crescent* near Alexandria, Virginia.

Overnight hotshot. Pennsylvania eastbound tonnage on the Fort Wayne division.

Westbound climb. Union Pacific Extra 8444 on Sherman Hill, Wyoming.

Sheltered view. CNR #6218 on the Grand Trunk Western near Valparaiso, Indiana.

After a day's work. Burlington Railroad at Fairmont, Nebraska.

Repetitious patterns. B&O eastbound coal train near Keyser, West Virginia.

Ready tracks. New York Central at Harmon, New York.

To and from the mines. Virginian Railway at Roanoke, Virginia.

Shop buildings. Illinois Central Railroad at Waterloo, Iowa.

The operator's view. Amtrak GG1 and E-60 on the Cos Cob, Connecticut, draw.

Contours of power. Ex–Texas & Pacific 2-10-4 #610.

Servicing stop. Reading Railroad at Shamokin, Pennsylvania.

First-generation Geeps. Boston & Maine southbound through Charlestown, New Hampshire.

Kansas City Power & Light unit train on the Union Pacific near Lawrence, Kansas.

Wheels and axles. Western Pacific at Portola, California.

First trick off duty. Southern Pacific at Bakersfield, California.

New Haven Railroad's steel and electric architecture at Norwalk, Connecticut.

Preceding pages
The Shenandoah division and the main line. B&O at Harpers Ferry.

New Haven Railroad's steel and electric architecture at Norwalk, Connecticut.

Preceding pages
The Shenandoah division and the main line. B&O at Harpers Ferry.

Electric articulation. New York Central at North White Plains, New York.

Under Park Avenue. Grand Central Terminal, New York.

Snow flurries and solitude. Norfolk & Western at Portsmouth yard, Ohio.

Contrasts in age. Union Pacific gas turbine at Cheyenne, Wyoming.

South Norwalk, Connecticut interlocking on the former New Haven Railroad.

Hackensack River draw. Erie Railroad train to Port Jervis, New York.

Sparrows Point trestle. Western Maryland Railway at Baltimore, Maryland.

New York Central's *20th Century Limited* departing Harmon, New York.

Heading for Duluth. Great Northern's *Gopher* at Superior, Wisconsin.

Amtrak's *San Francisco Zephyr* descending Donner Pass, California.

Nocturnal languish. Chesapeake & Ohio's train no. 48 at Lee Hall, Virginia.

The ides of winter. Chicago & Northwestern at River Forest, Illinois.

Connecticut River fog. Green Mountain Railroad northbound through Riverside, Vermont.

New Haven Railroad's Danbury branch. Norwalk, Connecticut.

Lehigh & Hudson River train departing Warwick, New York.

Soo Line departing Schiller Park, Illinois, northbound.

Urban landmarks. Penn Central local at Croxton, New Jersey.

Amtrak's *Southwestern Limited* departing Chicago.

At the century mark. D.C. bound Amtrak Metroliner in New Jersey.

Turbo along the Hudson. Amtrak at Roa's Hook, New York.

Burlington Northern eastbound hotshot near Naperville, Illinois.

Meet on Horseshoe Curve. Amtrak's *National Limited*, eastbound.

Spring morning. New Haven westbound at Cos Cob, Connecticut.

The ubiquitous switcher. Kansas City Terminal Railway.

The climb up Cajon on the Union Pacific.

Winter storm. Chicago & Northwestern in Chicago.

Chicago, South Shore & South Bend activity near Kensington, Indiana.

Penn Central U-boat laying over at Danbury, Connecticut.

Santa Fe stored power at Argentine Yards—Kansas City, Kansas.

The road freight and the switcher. Union Pacific at Topeka, Kansas.

Union Pacific eastbound at Midland, Kansas.

Yarmouth Junction, Maine, on the Maine Central and Grand Trunk.

Santa Fe Alcos climbing Cajon Pass at Summit, California.

Relic of the past. Rock Island interlocking tower at Saginaw, Texas.

Southern Pacific extra 4449 at Grass Valley, California.

Extra 4449 west on the Burlington Northern along the Columbia River.

Penn Central yard goat. Sunnyside Yards—Long Island City, New York.

Jack Shaft electrics on the Virginian Railway at Elmore, West Virginia.

Nature and man. Northwestern Steel & Wire at Sterling, Illinois.

Switch stand. Monon Railroad near Monon, Indiana.

Horseshoe climb. Penn Central westbound coal train west of Altoona, Pennsylvania.

Northern Pacific Railway telegraph office at De Smet, Montana.

Sentinels. Union Pacific west of Lawrence, Kansas.

Texas grass fire along the Santa Fe. Trinity River, Texas.

Derelict. Elk River Coal & Lumber 2-8-2 at Dundon, West Virginia.

Out of service. Passenger coach at Rockingham, Vermont.

Railroad bone yard. Baltimore, Maryland.

Abandoned stone quarry. New York Central at Little Stony Point, New York.